EARTHQUAKES

EARTHQUAKES

PETER MURRAY
THE CHILD'S WORLD®

On January 17, 1994, the people of Los Angeles woke up at exactly 4:31 A.M.

One man said, "I thought a giant had crawled under my bed and started shaking it up and down." Dishes fell from cupboards, bookcases crashed to the floor, and windowpanes popped from their frames. Every car alarm in the city started howling. Gas lines and water pipes were torn open. People ran from their homes, afraid that their ceilings would collapse. The shaking lasted only forty seconds, but it seemed like much longer.

Earthquakes always do.

Think of Earth as a hard-boiled egg with the shell cracked, but not peeled off. Beneath our feet lies the *crust*, a layer of cool, hard rock about sixty miles thick. The crust is made up of enormous *crustal plates,* thousands of miles across. The crustal plates fit together like pieces in a jigsaw puzzle.

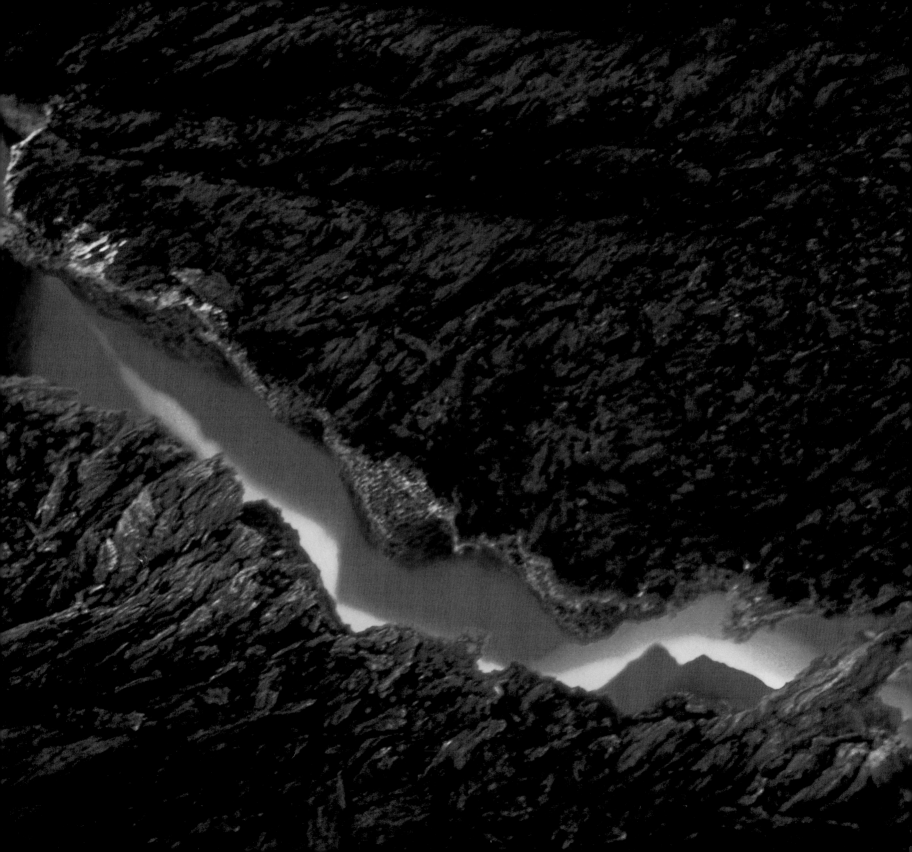

Beneath the crust lies a layer of hot, half-molten rock called the *mantle.* The crustal plates float like rafts on this ocean of soft stone, pushing against each other and pulling apart. They move so slowly that they might take a hundred years to travel an inch. Sometimes, though, they move a little faster.

When crustal plates pull apart or press together, tremendous forces build up. Sometimes the plates slip and move so suddenly we can feel the earth shift beneath our feet. When the earth moves suddenly and violently, we call it an earthquake.

A *fault* is a crack in the earth's crust. Most faults occur at the seams between crustal plates. The San Andreas fault in California lies at the boundary of the Pacific Ocean plate and the North American plate. Most faults are hidden deep underground, but the San Andreas fault reaches all the way to the surface.

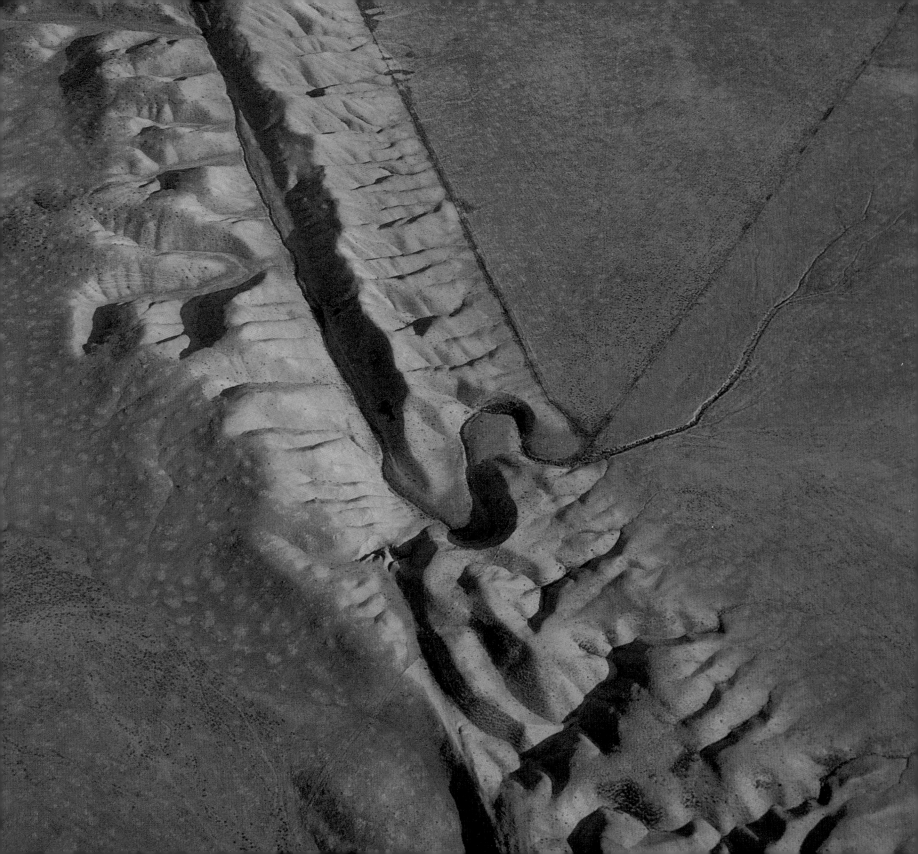

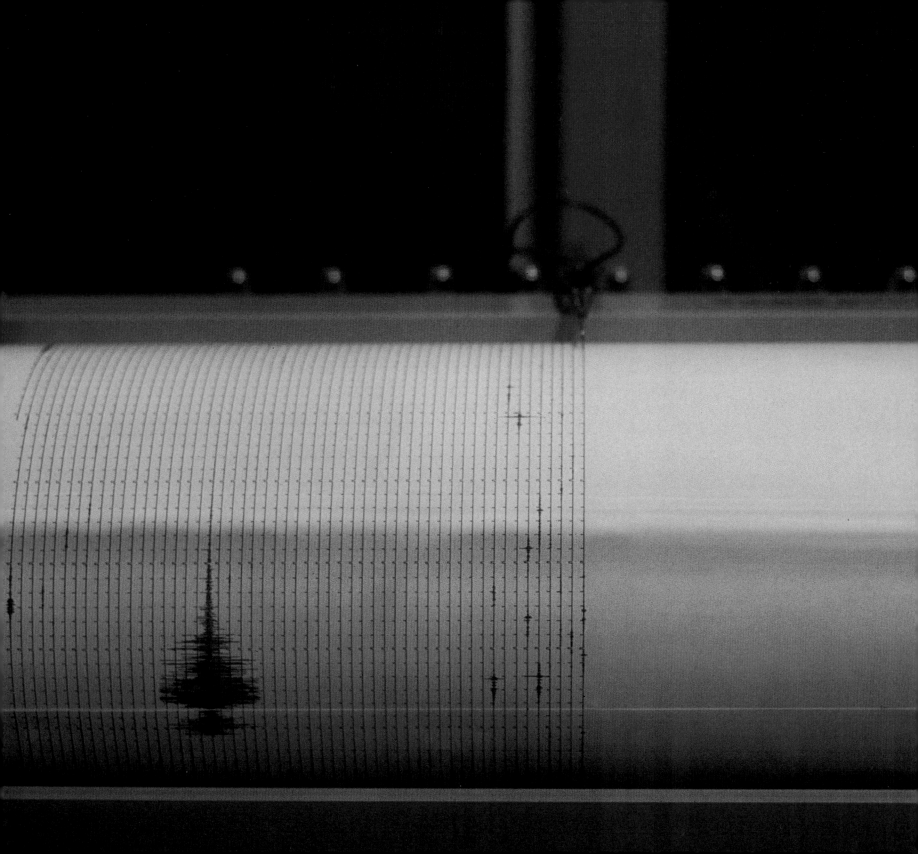

Scientists use machines called *seismographs* to detect and measure tiny movements in the earth's crust. A seismograph in Kansas can feel the vibrations from an earthquake in Los Angeles! Seismographs and other instruments help us learn more about what lies beneath our feet.

When an earthquake happens right under your feet, you don't need a machine to tell you that the ground is shaking. You know!

By using seismographs located in different parts of the world, scientists can locate an earthquake's *epicenter*. The epicenter is the place beneath the earth where the quake started. Usually, the worst earthquake damage is directly above the epicenter.

In the Los Angeles earthquake of 1994, the epicenter was directly below the suburb of Northridge. Damage from the quake spread for many miles, but the people living in Northridge suffered the worst destruction. One apartment building collapsed, burying sixteen people. A freeway buckled and twisted and fell apart. In nearby San Fernando, an oil pipe exploded, destroying dozens of buildings.

Fifty-five people died in the Los Angeles earthquake. That seems like a lot of people, but it could have been worse. In 1556, an earthquake in China killed 830,000 people. The Tokyo earthquake of 1923 took 143,000 lives and destroyed over half a million buildings.

Most earthquakes do little or no damage. There are about 6,000 earthquakes every year—700 in the United States—but only a few cause serious damage. People living in earthquake zones get used to the small, harmless quakes. But they never stop worrying about the big ones.

One of the strongest earthquakes ever recorded struck Anchorage, Alaska, in 1964. The Kenai Peninsula—including the entire town of Anchorage—sank seven feet. The area just to the south was raised by as much as ten feet. The Anchorage quake measured 8.5 on the *Richter scale*.

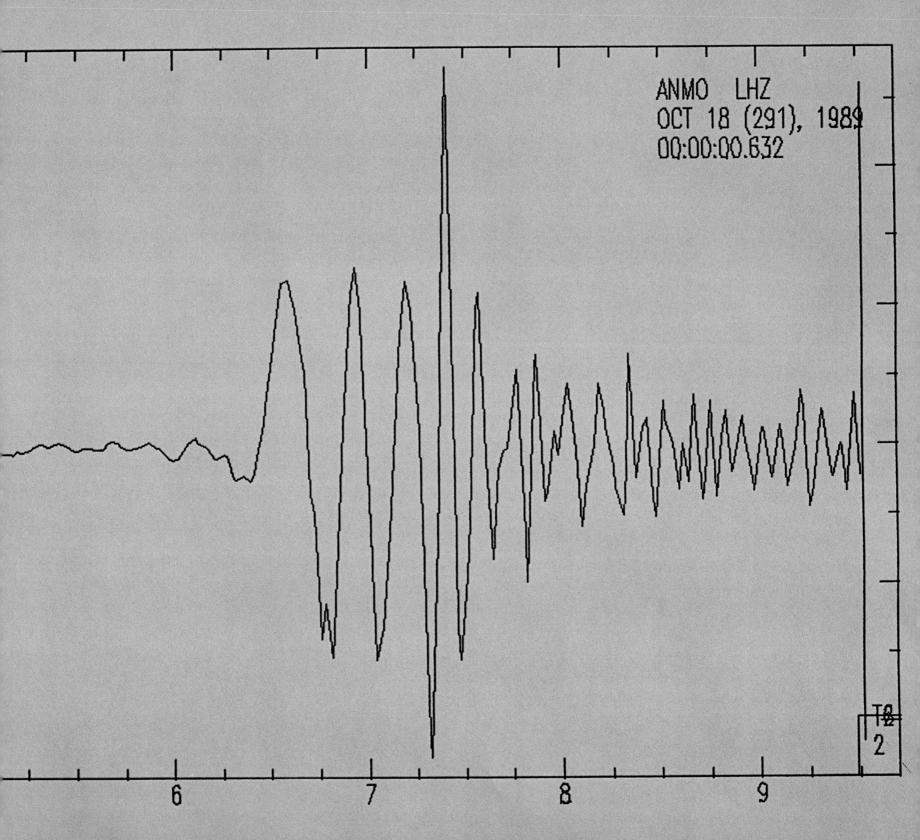

The Richter scale is a way of estimating the strength of an earthquake. The weakest tremors we can feel measure about 2 on the Richter scale. Anything over 6 is considered a strong earthquake. The Los Angeles earthquake of 1994 measured 6.5 on the Richter scale.

Earthquakes can cause avalanches, falling buildings, and cracks in the earth, but the most deadly of all earthquake effects is the *tsunami*. When a section of the earth's crust beneath the ocean suddenly rises or falls, an enormous wave can form. This tsunami travels quickly, sometimes over 100 miles per hour. As the tsunami approaches land it grows larger, reaching heights of up to 100 feet.

The Alaskan earthquake produced a series of tsunami that struck the coast from British Columbia all the way down to Mexico. Even the Hawaiian Islands—3,000 miles away—were hit by thirty-foot waves!

If an earthquake strikes, it helps to know what to do. The first thing you should do when a quake strikes is go outside. Most injuries are caused by falling objects like bookshelves, light fixtures, or collapsing walls. Go to an open area and stay there. Watch out for fallen power lines and shattered glass. When the shaking stops, don't go back inside! Earthquakes are often followed by smaller quakes called *aftershocks*. Aftershocks can cause weakened buildings to collapse.

Most of all, stay calm. There is nothing you can do to stop the earthquake, so don't try.

In California people talk about "The Big One." The Big One is the earthquake that hasn't happened yet. It's the earthquake that everyone fears will come when the forces building along the San Andreas fault suddenly give way.

No one knows for sure what the future will bring. There may not be another major earthquake for years. The Big One might never happen. Or maybe it will come tomorrow.

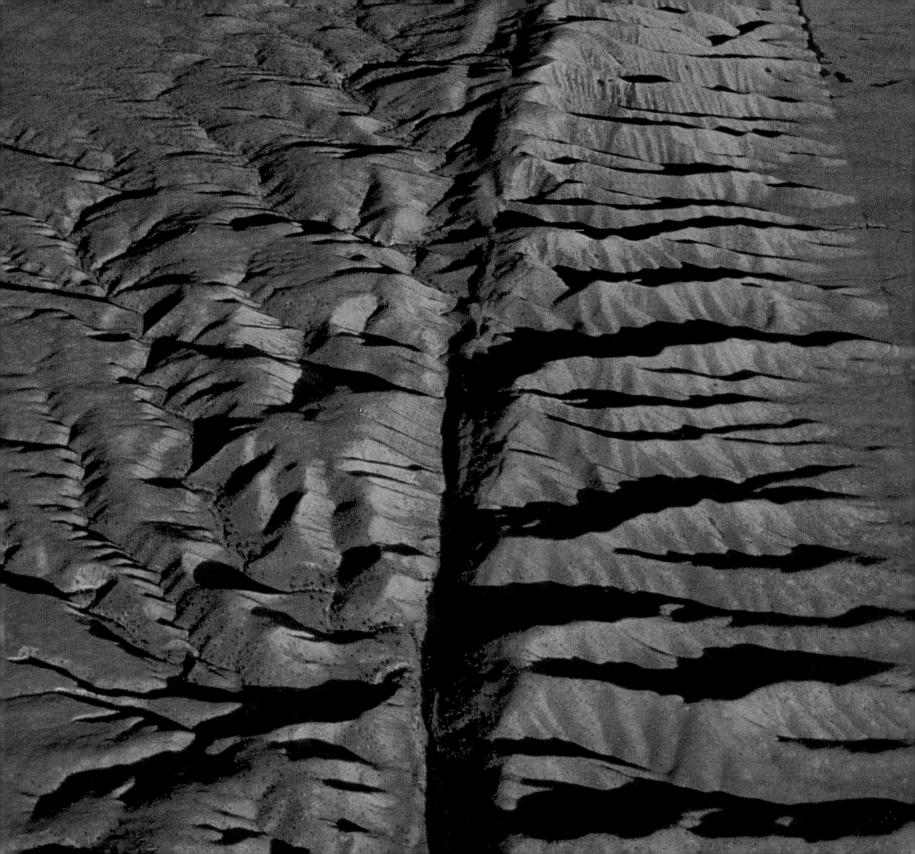

INDEX

PHOTO RESEARCH
Kristee Flynn

PHOTO CREDITS
TONY STONE / Andrew Rafkind: cover
COMSTOCK / Georg Gerster: 2, 7, 13
COMSTOCK / Bonnie Kamin: 11
COMSTOCK / Mike & Carol Werner: 14
SCIENCE PHOTO LIBRARY / David Parker: 4
SCIENCE PHOTO LIBRARY / U.S. Geological
Survey: 22
PHOTO RESEARCHERS / Ket M. Krafft / Explorer: 8
PHOTO RESEARCHERS / David Weintraub: 18
PHOTO RESEARCHERS / Tom McHugh: 28
PHOTO RESEARCHERS / Francois Gohier: 31
Warren Faidley / WEATHERSTOCK: 17, 24
Nita Winter: 21
D. Olsen / WEATHERSTOCK: 27

Library of Congress Cataloging-in-Publication Data
Murray, Peter, 1952 Sept. 29-
Earthquakes / by Peter Murray.
p. cm.
Includes Index.
ISBN 1-56766-198-X

1. Earthquakes--Juvenile literature. [1. Earthquakes.] I. Title.
QE521.3.M87 1995 95-3516
581.2'2--dc20